LONDON
A VIEW FROM THE
THAMES

The Thames at Richmond

GRACIOUS LIVING – HAMPTON COURT TO RICHMOND BRIDGE

Between Hampton Court and Richmond Bridge the Thames passes through leafy suburbs studded with gracious houses. Historically these reaches were favoured for the building of homes for the aristocracy, far from the noise and smells of the city but within speedy reach of the capital by boat.

Hampton Court is the most magnificent of the mansions, but Ham House, Orleans House and Strawberry Hill are other architectural gems. All are set in parks which stretch down to the river and create the rural ambience so characteristic of this part of the Thames.

Kingston and Richmond, once bustling towns in their own right, have long since been swallowed up by London, yet still maintain a busy and important air.

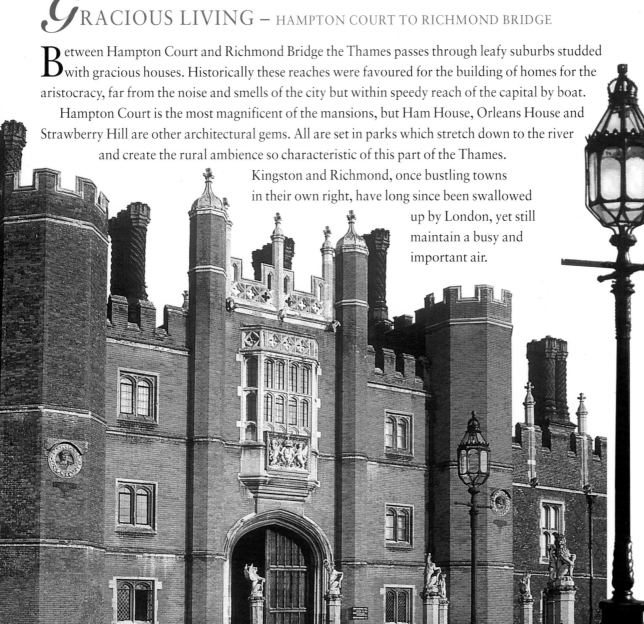

Making a grand entrance

Hampton Court's main entrance, the Trophy Gate, was part of Cardinal Wolsey's grandiose conception and fully succeeds in its intention to impress. The roundels on the turrets depict Roman emperors, while heraldic beasts flank the central archway.

A palace twice over

With its thousand rooms, the great, red-brick, rambling palace of Hampton Court is more a small town than a house. It was built in two main phases: Wolsey and Henry VIII between them created the original Tudor palace with its battlemented walls and ornate, twisted chimneys, and William III commissioned Christopher Wren to add new state apartments in the classical style, as well as laying out the vast formal gardens. Tudor and baroque palaces survive together, a marvellously imposing whole.

Times change

The magnificent astrological clock at Hampton Court was designed in 1540, before the discoveries of Galileo and Copernicus proved that the earth revolves around the sun; the symbols in its centre are the sun in its progress around the earth. The clock, restored to its original colour, displays a wealth of additional useful information: the hour, date, month, number of days from the beginning of the year, signs of the zodiac, phases of the moon, and the time of high tide at London Bridge.

Puzzling gardens

Shrieks of laughter and frustration drift across Hampton Court's gardens from visitors lost in its famous maze, planted more than two and a half centuries ago in the reign of Queen Anne. The gardens have been embellished and redesigned by successive monarchs over the years, most notably by William III, whose formal gardens to the east of the palace have recently been restored. A gigantic vine planted in 1769 is still flourishing.

From cottage to castle

Strawberry Hill bears the stamp of two remarkable people – Horace Walpole, the eighteenth-century writer who bought a small villa set back from the river in Twickenham, and Frances, Countess Waldegrave, who inherited the house in 1846. He added pinnacles, quatrefoil windows and other medieval conceits all over the enlarged house. She added more battlements – and even extended the railway to her door. The result is an exuberant homage to the Gothic which was enormously influential, giving rise to an architectural style called Strawberry Hill Gothic.

Water sprites in Twickenham

In the gardens of York House, Twickenham, naked white nymphs cavort among the lily leaves and trickling streams. They grace a remarkable fountain installed by the Indian merchant prince Sir Ratan Tata, who lived here in the early years of this century. The house has had many owners since it was built in the late seventeenth century, including the exiled French royal family. Now housing civic offices, York House may be visited by arrangement with the nearby tourist office, though the gardens are permanently open.

A gift for the whipping boy

Situated in glorious parkland beside the Thames, Ham House has changed little since the seventeenth century. Built in 1610, the house was acquired in 1637 by William Murray, first Earl of Dysart, who in his childhood had been 'whipping boy' for the future Charles I, a post which entailed being punished in place of the prince for any royal misdemeanour. His early sufferings were later rewarded by the gift of the manors of Ham and Petersham.

A literary landscape

In 1724 Henrietta Howard, the mistress of the Prince of Wales (later George II), decided that she needed her own residence. Five years and £11,500 of royal money later, a handsome Palladian-style villa known as Marble Hill House was erected on the banks of the river in Twickenham. To make the most of the view she enlisted the services of friend, neighbour and poet Alexander Pope to help design the parkland.

Eighteenth-century eulogy

'Heavens! What a goodly prospect spreads around, of hills, and dales, and woods, and lawn and spires and glittering towns and gilded streams.' So enthused James Thomson of Richmond Hill in 1727. His description, though well over two and a half centuries old, is valid to this day. The small island in the Thames is Glover Island.

THE RURAL HEART OF LONDON
RICHMOND BRIDGE TO CHISWICK BRIDGE

Though little more than seven miles from the centre of London, stretches of the Thames between Richmond and Chiswick bridges give the impression of being in the depths of the English countryside.

In one section, downstream from Isleworth, hardly a building can be seen for almost a mile; Kew Gardens on one side and Syon Park on the other give the riverside the look and feel of the country, with willows dipping into the water and herons standing lugubriously in the tidal mudflats. The distant view of Syon House and the peaceful, village-like river frontages of Isleworth and the Strand on the Green are in full accord with this tranquil scene.

Remnants of medieval forests

Many of the mightier oaks in Richmond Park are remnants of the huge forests which once surrounded the capital. Conveniently close by river to Hampton Court, the park is a former hunting ground of Charles I, and there are herds of red and fallow deer to this day. The park also contains some fine gardens, such as the Isabella Plantation, a blaze of colour in late spring when the azaleas and rhododendrons are at their finest.

Riverside tranquillity

Isleworth was once a peaceful riverside village known as Gristlesworde. Turner, Constable and Zoffany all painted this quiet stretch of the Thames.

Opulent interiors

Syon House contains some of the most magnificently decorated rooms in England. When in 1762 the Earl of Northumberland found his home to be 'ruinous and inconvenient' he employed Robert Adam to design a sumptuous set of apartments within the shell of the original building. This, the ante-room, is lavishly gilded in Roman style with green columns and a brilliantly coloured scagliola floor.

A troubled history

The rather forbidding frontage of Syon House faces the Thames across its rolling park. Still the seat of the dukes of Northumberland, it is the only house in London to have remained in hereditary ownership for over 400 years. Originally a convent, Syon was seized by Henry VIII at the dissolution of the monasteries and was used as a prison for his wife, Catherine Howard, before her execution. After Henry died it was given to the Duke of Somerset who converted it into the Tudor mansion which stands today.

Gardens under glass

The fragile transparent dome of Syon's Great Conservatory contrasts with the solid castellations of the house itself. Built in the 1820s and said to be the model for the Crystal Palace, the conservatory contains a variety of different plant habitats and is one of the most exciting features of Syon's distinguished gardens. Other attractions include a magnificent rose garden, a well-stocked garden centre, a butterfly house and the largest collection of historic British cars in the world.

A worldwide reputation

The serious work of collecting unusual and exotic plants at Kew was instigated by Princess Augusta on a small nine-acre site near the royal palace. Under her son, George III, the gardens were enlarged and became established as one of the world's foremost centres for horticultural research, a reputation which they still enjoy. The gardens now spread over more than 300 acres. Kew's great greenhouses were constructed after the gardens were handed over to the state in 1841. The celebrated Palm House is composed of curved sheets of glass and contains a profusion of hothouse plants.

The royals' rural idyll

The most modest of royal residences, Kew Palace began life in 1631 as a Dutch merchant's house. It was leased by Queen Caroline in 1728 'for the rent of £100 and a fat doe' and thereafter was used by various members of the royal family as a refreshing change from the glitter of the London court. George III, in particular, loved to come here, and the house remains as it was in his time.

A taste of the Orient

Kew Gardens were originally conceived as a royal pleasure ground and in the time of George III were dotted with quirky summer-houses and follies. Of these only a handful remain, including the Great Pagoda, designed in 1761 by William Chambers who had visited China in his youth. Once elaborately decorated, it is now a relatively simple structure ten storeys high.

Cricket on the green

On Saturday and Sunday afternoons between May and September Kew Green is a venue for one of the most quintessentially English and – to the foreign visitor – baffling of pastimes. Cricket is played on many a village green all over the country, but few can be as beautiful as this. Fine, late-eighteenth-century Georgian houses surround the cricket pitch, which is also overlooked by St Anne's Church. St Anne's contains a pleasing vaulted ceiling and the tombs of two eighteenth-century English artists, Thomas Gainsborough and John Zoffany.

Alight here for Kew Gardens

The Strand on the Green, a row of particularly fine eighteenth-century houses on the northern bank of the Thames, is the backdrop to a pleasureboat moored at Kew Pier. The famous Kew Gardens are just a short walk away.

Outdated but not outworn

At weekends, the old pumping station near Kew Bridge resounds with the clanking of pistons and the hissing of steam. The great beam engines, the largest of their kind in the world, pumped millions of gallons of water to the homes of west London until newer technology overtook them. Still in working order and operated at weekends, they form the main exhibits of the Kew Bridge Steam Museum, dedicated to steam-driven machines of all varieties.

ATTRACTED BY THE FISH

That the Thames is once again a clean and healthy river is most visible from the large numbers of birds living on or beside it. They are attracted by the considerable fish population – no fewer than 114 species are thought to inhabit the Thames. So it is not surprising to find grey herons and cormorants on a trip upstream, but what *is* surprising is to see them in such profusion, used to the noise and commotion of the river and its craft. The largest and most elegant of the resident birds are the mute swans. Canada geese are a common sight, as are mallards, moorhens and coots. Near Richmond Park you may also catch sight of the appealing tufted ducks or the beautiful great crested grebes. In spring very young grebes, all fluffy stripes, are often carried on their parents' backs in an attempt to protect them from underwater predators such as the pike.

Grey heron

Boats on the River
CHISWICK BRIDGE TO WANDSWORTH BRIDGE

Chiswick Bridge marks the finishing point of the University Boat Race, and at all times of the year the famous double bend of the Thames downstream from Chiswick Bridge is definitely rowing territory. Rowing eights – and fours and twos – dodge the pleasure boats as they practise their strokes, the shouts of coxes reverberate across the water, and the banks of the river through Barnes and Chiswick are dotted with boathouses.

Here Chiswick presents a particularly civilised face to the Thames, with Upper and Lower Malls lined with gracious houses. Downstream from Harrod's Depository the river scene becomes more urban, relieved by the green parks of Fulham Palace and Hurlingham House, as the Thames nears the busy heart of the city.

Sir Joseph Bazalgette's bridge

The present Hammersmith Bridge was built by the master engineer Sir Joseph Bazalgette in 1883–7. The coats of arms on the pillars at its entrance are often erroneously believed to be Canadian in origin, but they actually include the crests of Kent (the horse), the old county of Middlesex (the three swords), the town of Guildford in Surrey (the castle and lion) and the defunct Metropolitan Board of Works (whose chief engineer was Sir Joseph).

UNIVERSITY CHALLENGE

The boat race between Oxford and Cambridge universities, rowed every year on a Saturday close to Easter, is still the big event of the Thames. In Victorian times the race was so popular that racegoers swarmed to Putney often a week before the race itself, and the riverside took on the atmosphere of a fairground. When the great day arrived the banks, pubs, bridges and trees would be packed with spectators and the river would be full of steamers and private boats jostling for prime position. Today, with the race being televised, something of the festival atmosphere has gone but it still attracts the crowds. The teams row four-and-a-half miles from Putney to Mortlake, Oxford in dark blue and Cambridge in light blue.

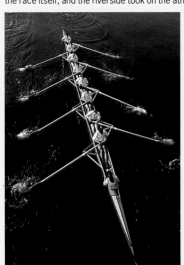

The Oxford/Cambridge Chiswick bridge marker

A concrete tent

In the churchyard of St Mary Magdalene, Mortlake, is an extraordinary tomb. Standing amidst the undergrowth, is a 5.5-metre-high concrete Arabian tent, the last resting place of explorer Sir Richard Burton and his wife Isabel. A small window in the tent's roof affords a glimpse of the two sarcophagi.

Art before comfort

White, pure and severely classical, Chiswick House was not designed for comfortable living. It was built rather as a temple to the arts and as the supreme example of Palladian architecture in England. Its creator, the third Earl of Burlington, one of the first English aristocrats to make the Grand Tour of Europe, was so impressed by the classical villas of northern Italy that he commissioned his friend, the architect William Kent, to design a mansion for him in similar style. Modelled on Palladio's Villa Rotonda at Vicenza and completed in 1729, it housed the earl's works of art and was used for entertaining his eminent friends, but he continued to live next door in his much more comfortable old Jacobean home, since demolished.

Riverside elegance

The waterfront stretching from Kew Bridge to Hammersmith Bridge provides some of the most picturesque scenery of London's Thames. The peaceful riverside lanes and pavements of Chiswick Mall, Upper Mall and Lower Mall are backed by elegant seventeenth- and eighteenth-century houses, some with ornate balconies and fanlights, others with quiet gardens stretching down to the river.

Italianate gardens

When William Kent designed the gardens at Chiswick House he set out to break the mould of English garden design. Instead of the geometric arrangements of the Renaissance formal garden, he surrounded the Palladian mansion with Italianate grounds to match, attempting to create an idealised classical landscape dotted with temples, statues and obelisks.

Home of a remarkable Englishman

Kelmscott House at Upper Mall, Hammersmith, was the London home of the poet, designer and craftsman William Morris from 1877 until his death in 1896. Here he set up the Kelmscott Press, dedicated to the fine printing of hand-illustrated books. It is now the headquarters of the William Morris Society.

London's little-known palace

For about 900 years, from the eleventh century until 1973, quiet and peaceful Fulham Palace was the official residence of the bishops of London. Now, though, this part-sixteenth-century house, set back slightly from the river, welcomes visitors to its twin courtyards and extensive grounds, stocked with a variety of rare trees.

APPROACHING LONDON'S HEART

WANDSWORTH BRIDGE TO LAMBETH BRIDGE

The increasing frequency of ornate nineteenth-century bridges on this stretch of the river indicates that the Thames is approaching the busy, bustling hub of London. Even so, the first stretch through the old part of Chelsea retains an elegant residential feel; Cheyne Walk, home to so many of England's nineteenth-century artistic and social élite, presents its graceful frontage to the river. Not far away, though, two mighty power stations, Lots Road and the now defunct Battersea, are signs that the river is becoming more industrial and commercial. Chelsea Hospital, home to the famous Chelsea Pensioners, is the first of the grandiose public buildings which begin to line the riverbanks.

Divided loyalties

A window in St Mary's Church, Battersea, is dedicated to Benedict Arnold, a name which in America is synonymous with treachery. Arnold began as a general in Washington's army during the American Civil War, serving with outstanding courage and panache, but before hostilities were over he had defected to the British side. Afterwards he returned to live in London and he is buried in St Mary's Church – no one knows quite why, as his home was in Brompton.

High tide for all to see

The modern development of shops, offices, restaurants, apartments and a hotel, together known as Chelsea Harbour, has at its centre a block of flats called the Belvedere. It provides for its occupants stupendous views of London and like the Old Royal Observatory at Greenwich, has on its apex a large globe fixed to a rod. Instead of enabling mariners to reset their chronometers, as at Greenwich, the position of this golden ball indicates the state of the tide.

A graceful hybrid

Decked with strings of light at night, Albert Bridge at Chelsea is a curious mixture of cantilever structure and a suspension bridge. The overall effect is highly decorative, making it one of the most distinctive and charming of London's upstream bridges. It was once a tollbridge and the tollbooths are still in place at either end of its span.

Peace pagoda

A prominent landmark on the south bank, this Buddhist pagoda was erected in Battersea Park in 1985. A symbol of peace, it stands, slightly ironically, on land famed until Victorian times for its lawlessness. Formerly known as Battersea Fields, it was the haunt of London's riff-raff and a territory for illegal duelling. Its most famous duel was in 1829 between the Duke of Wellington and Lord Winchilsea – neither received a scratch.

Monument to power

One of the most distinctive – and some would say distinguished – buildings on the southern bank of the Thames is Battersea Power Station. The vast brick building was designed by an architect who relished working on the grand scale, Sir Giles Gilbert Scott. First generating electricity in 1933, the power station sent smoke up its four ninety-metre-high fluted chimneys for exactly fifty years until it closed in 1983. Plans to turn the building into a theme park ran out of steam in 1991.

Hospital for heroes

Christopher Wren chose the site beside the Thames for the Royal Hospital at Chelsea, which was completed in 1692. It was his first full-scale secular commission after rebuilding so many churches destroyed during the Great Fire. Chelsea Hospital still performs the function for which it was designed, housing some 500 army pensioners who wear a distinctive uniform of navy blue overcoats in winter and scarlet frock-coats in summer.

An oasis of tranquillity

The Chelsea Physic Garden was established in 1676 by the Apothecaries Company with the aim of researching the medicinal properties of plants, an intention which is pursued to this day. Apart from familiar medicinal and culinary herbs, it contains within its sheltering brick walls exotic trees and flowers collected from around the world, among them the tallest olive tree in Britain.

Apollo the healer

Anyone entering Chelsea Physic Garden through its river gate – now, sadly, some distance from the Thames – would have passed beneath this magnificent sign. The badge of the Worshipful Society of Apothecaries, it shows the sun god Apollo in his capacity as healer of the sick, standing astride the dragon of disease. The crest is a rhinoceros – the horn of this beast was supposed to have miraculous curative properties.

STREET OF FAME

Chelsea's romantic and artistic reputation was cemented in the nineteenth century, when the elegant Queen Anne houses of Cheyne Walk attracted more eminent figures than perhaps any other single street in the country. The painter J M W Turner moved to No. 119 when already famous, living there until his death in 1851 under the assumed name of Booth to guard his privacy. In 1862 the Pre-Raphaelite artist and poet Dante Gabriel Rossetti took No. 16, one of the most imposing houses in the street, where he entertained his artistic friends – and installed a small menagerie. The cries of the peacocks were so unpopular with his neighbours that the birds were expressly forbidden under subsequent leases of the property. Later, James McNeil Whistler spent twelve productive years at No. 96 painting some of his finest works, and from No. 109 another artist, Philip Wilson Steer, would walk through Chelsea accompanied by a large cat.

Among Cheyne Walk's literary residents, Mrs Gaskell was born at No. 93, George Eliot died at No. 4, Henry James lived until his death at Carlyle Mansions and Hilaire Belloc spent four years at No. 104. To the long list of literary and artistic greats may be added two from the world of engineering: from No. 98 Sir Marc Brunel planned the Rotherhithe Tunnel, the first underwater tunnel ever built; his son, the famous Isambard Kingdom Brunel, was just a small child at the time.

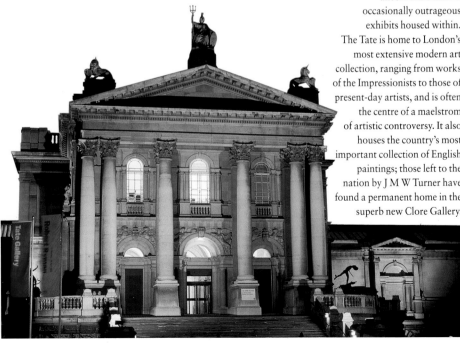

The English and the avant-garde

The classical facade of the Tate Gallery does little to prepare the visitor for some of the unconventional and occasionally outrageous exhibits housed within. The Tate is home to London's most extensive modern art collection, ranging from works of the Impressionists to those of present-day artists, and is often the centre of a maelstrom of artistic controversy. It also houses the country's most important collection of English paintings; those left to the nation by J M W Turner have found a permanent home in the superb new Clore Gallery.

The building with no name

This magnificent post-modernist building overlooking the Thames by Vauxhall Bridge has no official name. Designed in 1990–92 by Terry Farrell, a leading figure in the British post-modernist movement, it houses MI6, the arm of the British intelligence service concerned with foreign espionage.

LONDON'S POWER BASE
LAMBETH BRIDGE TO WATERLOO BRIDGE

Power and importance are the hallmarks of this section of the Thames, the site of some of the most significant buildings in the country. Just below Lambeth Bridge the centres of ecclesiastical and political power in England face one another across the water. Lambeth Palace, official residence of the Archbishop of Canterbury, the head of the Church of England, looks directly across to the neo-Gothic facade of the Houses of Parliament, home of the country's parliamentary democracy.

Further on, great buildings of state rise up from the Embankment – County Hall, the Ministry of Defence and the former Scotland Yard – interspersed with some equally imposing company headquarters. Here, too, is the hub of London's cultural scene, the South Bank Centre, housing some of the best of the nation's theatres, concert halls and galleries.

The scourge of the Romans

Magnificently sited below the Palace of Westminster's clock tower – popularly known as Big Ben after the clock's bell – is a statue of Boudicca, the bellicose queen of the Iceni tribe, who were based roughly in present-day Norfolk. In AD 60 she and her marauding tribespeople razed the Roman town of Londinium to the ground. Her bronze likeness was cast in the 1850s by Thomas Thornycroft.

Gothic extravagance

One of London's many disastrous fires destroyed the old Palace of Westminster in 1834. Charles Barry was awarded the huge task of reconstruction, and immediately teamed up with Augustus Pugin, the noted expert on Gothic ornamentation. The resulting palace – usually known as the Houses of Parliament – is one of the most ebullient of Gothic creations, best seen from the Albert Embankment or the river.

Rugged determination

Stooped in naval coat and leaning on a stick, the familiar form of Sir Winston Churchill looks towards Big Ben from Parliament Square. The very picture of dogged tenacity, Churchill led Britain for most of the war years, returning to the post of prime minister in 1951. His presence beside the Houses of Parliament is especially apt, since among countless other achievements he notched up no fewer than sixty-three years as an MP, more than any other parliamentarian.

The Archbishop's pied-à-terre

Since 1190 Lambeth Palace has been the official London home of the Archbishop of Canterbury, head of the Anglican Church. The extensive complex of buildings has had a busy history; during the Commonwealth period, the eleven years in the seventeenth century when England was without a monarch, the Tudor gatehouse next to the tower of the Church of St Mary was used as a prison while the chapel was used by parliamentarian soldiers for the uncharacteristic business of dancing.

Graves and gardens

Admiral Bligh, of the famous mutiny ship the *Bounty*, was a keen collector of plants and would have approved of his tomb at St Mary at Lambeth Church being surrounded by an array of colourful and exotic flowers and shrubs. The church, now redundant, houses the Museum of Garden History in honour of John Tradescant, famous botanist and gardener for Charles I, who is also buried here. Tradescant brought many plants to Britain, including the lilac, jasmine and larch, and is probably responsible for introducing the pineapple as a decorative motif in England – hence the golden pineapples at the ends of nearby Lambeth Bridge.

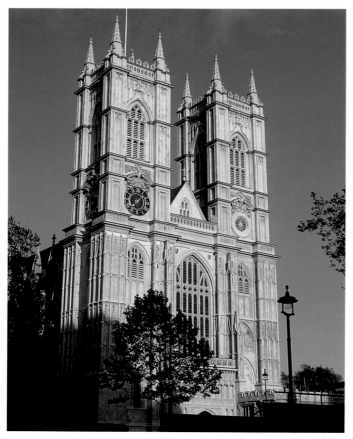

A modest request

The playwright Ben Jonson's monument in Poets' Corner in Westminster Abbey has the same brief epitaph as the stone marking his burial place in the nave (*above*) – and it reflects the modesty of his burial request: 'Six feet long by two feet wide is too much for me; two by two will do for all I want.' Accordingly, he was buried upright!

Hawksmoor's twin towers

The soaring west towers of Westminster Abbey were relatively late additions to the otherwise mainly medieval building. It was begun in 1245 by Henry III as a shrine to his royal predecessor and saint, Edward the Confessor, and was finished, apart from the upper parts of the west towers, by 1532. Not until the eighteenth century, however, did the task of adding the final touch to London's greatest church fall to Nicholas Hawksmoor; in 1745, almost 500 years after the building began, Westminster Abbey was complete.

Monuments to greatness

The splendid memorial to Isaac Newton is one of many in Westminster Abbey devoted to famous scientists and engineers. Once the burial place solely of England's kings and queens, the abbey began receiving the remains of commoners in the time of Richard II and is now crammed with tombs, monuments and plaques of all descriptions.

Intricate tracery

The exquisite fan vaulting of Henry VII's chapel at Westminster Abbey has been likened to the 'wonderful minuteness and airy security of a cobweb'. The chapel, built by the Tudor king in 1509, represents the last flowering of Perpendicular architecture in England; the tomb of Henry and his queen within the chapel is already in the later Renaissance style. The colourful array of banners suspended from the walls are those of the Knights of the Bath, whose inauguration ceremony is held here.

All aboard!

Some of the best views of London on a hot summer's day may be had from the deck of a Thames pleasure boat. Trips run from Westminster Pier upstream all the way to Hampton Court, and downstream as far as the Thames Barrier, with other embarkation points along the routes.

A kindly lion

The rather benign South Bank Lion has long been a feature of London's riverside. Erected in 1837 as the trademark for the Lion Brewery which once stood near Hungerford Bridge, it was preserved on the express wishes of George VI after the brewery was demolished in 1949, and moved to its present site some time afterwards. It is sculpted from a mysterious substance known as Coade Stone, an artificial type of terracotta almost impervious to weather. The lion can never be reconstructed, for the secret of making Coade Stone is now lost.

A view for eagle eyes

This memorial to officers of the RAF stands beside the Ministry of Defence. From its top a golden eagle glares across the Thames at the imposing edifice of County Hall opposite. Built to house local government offices, County Hall has lain empty since the controversial disbanding of the Greater London Council in 1986; plans are afoot to convert it into a luxury hotel and private apartments.

French château and Lincolnshire castle

The theatrical château rising behind the trees of the Victoria Embankment seems more in keeping with the banks of the Seine than the Thames. Built in 1884 to house a host of gentlemen's clubs, Whitehall Court is now a mixture of expensive apartments, a hotel and one surviving club, the Farmers'. By contrast, the paddle steamer moored in front is actually a Lincolnshire castle – at least in name. The Tattershall Castle is now a floating pub.

A buried era

The distinctive building looming large above Victoria Embankment Gardens is Shell Mex House, completed in 1931. In the foreground is Cleopatra's Needle, beneath which lies a Victorian time capsule, including a case of cigars, a railway timetable, four bibles in different languages and the portraits of twelve of England's most comely ladies. A twin obelisk stands in New York's Central Park.

Night-time drama

The eight-storey development of offices and shops above Charing Cross railway station was designed by Terry Farrell, leading proponent of the post-modernist style. This most elaborate of railway rooftops assumes its most dramatic aspect at night when, brightly floodlit, it takes on something of the air of a giant 1930s cinema.

Culture in concrete

In 1951, to mark the centenary of the Great Exhibition, London mounted the Festival of Britain in the hope of cheering people up after more than five years of post-war austerity. The Royal Festival Hall was the centrepiece of a complex of exhibition buildings devoted to the arts and sciences, and the only one intended as a permanent fixture. Its concrete shapes house a superb concert hall with marvellous acoustics. The siting of the Festival Hall provided the impetus for a number of other buildings devoted to the arts, known collectively as the South Bank Centre.

Bargains on the Embankment

The South Bank's reputation for culture spills over to the riverside pavement market – an excellent place to rummage for secondhand books.

Ancient and cumbersome

Roughly 3,500 years old, the pink granite obelisk known as Cleopatra's Needle is actually a monument to an obscure Egyptian pharaoh, Tethmosis III. Its unexpected presence on the north bank of the Thames is due to the Turkish rulers of Egypt presenting it to the British in 1819.

Thames vistas

The tree-lined riverside promenades in front of the South Bank Centre have fine views of the Thames skyline opposite, with the distinctive shape of the St Paul's Cathedral dome jostled by its surrounding array of fine buildings.

AUGUST AND ANCIENT INSTITUTIONS
WATERLOO BRIDGE TO SOUTHWARK BRIDGE

Grand facade

The splendidly imposing riverside facade of Somerset House fronts a building containing a mix of institutions including the Inland Revenue, the Principal Probate Registry and the Courtauld Gallery, home to some of the most distinguished Impressionist paintings in Britain. The late eighteenth-century building replaced another, equally grand, building on the site – the palace of Lord Protector Somerset, built in 1547–50. Until the Victoria Embankment was built the Thames lapped at the very foot of the building.

London's venerable history is writ large as the Thames meanders through the city's core. Standing defiant on the city skyline is the great dome of St Paul's Cathedral, survivor of the wartime blitz, hemmed in by the many new buildings of the City of London, Europe's financial centre. On the waterfront Vintners' Hall, headquarters of one of London's long-established livery companies, is a reminder that London's commercial history is as old as the city itself. Nearby, the Temple is home to another great institution, the legal profession, and on the opposite bank Shakespeare's famous Globe Theatre has been reconstructed anew.

Bazalgette's enduring monument

When in 1870 Sir Joseph Bazalgette embanked the northern side of the Thames between Westminster and Blackfriars bridges to form the Victoria Embankment, he managed to reclaim thirty-seven acres of prime land into the bargain. Much of this became the Victoria Embankment Gardens. The steep-roofed building to the left of St Paul's Cathedral is the former City of London School. Illustrious old boys include Sir Winston Churchill and authors Kingsley Amis and Julian Barnes.

London's legal hub

Home of lawyers, judges, barristers and of the legal profession in general, the Temple takes its name from the Knights Templar, an order of crusading knights in medieval Europe. With the extensive, turreted Royal Courts of Justice – usually known as the Law Courts – behind, here the Middle Temple can be seen in the foreground between the trees; the small, round tower of the Temple Church is in the lower right.

BAZALGETTE'S RIVER

One of London's great unsung heroes, Sir Joseph Bazalgette designed several of the capital's bridges – Albert, Battersea and Hammersmith bridges are all or partly his work – but his enduring achievements are the Victoria, Albert and Chelsea embankments, and London's drainage system.

The embankments were momentous structures: thirty-seven acres of mud were reclaimed and three-and-a-half miles faced with huge granite slabs. They were, however, nothing compared with the construction of London's sewers. In one outbreak of cholera in 1848-9, some 14,000 people died, and in the hot summer of 1858, known as the 'Great Stink', the Thames became so foul-smelling that the Houses of Parliament hung out sheets soaked with chloride of lime in an attempt to reduce the stench. In essence, the sewage of a population of about three million people was swept straight into the Thames. Sir Joseph Bazalgette's system of 1,300 miles of tunnel on three separate levels, together with elaborate pumping stations, was, on completion in 1875, the answer to this immense problem. Indeed it still is, for his civil-engineering triumph, unseen beneath the streets of London, remains the backbone of the capital's drainage system.

Cheating by design

The Oxo Tower stands on the south bank of the Thames between Waterloo and Blackfriars bridges. It was built in 1928 in an ingenious, and successful, attempt to circumvent a ban on outdoor advertising. The windows of the tower eloquently and attractively spell out the brand name of a well-known meat extract.

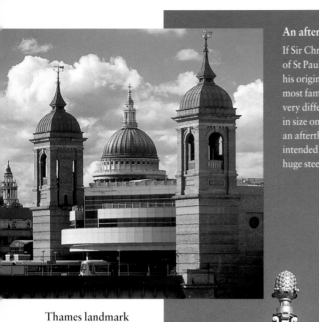

An afterthought

If Sir Christopher Wren, the architect of St Paul's Cathedral, had stuck to his original plans, one of London's most familiar landmarks would look very different. For the dome (second in size only to Rome's St Peter's) was an afterthought, as Wren had initially intended to crown the church with a huge steeple.

Thames landmark

The great dome of St Paul's Cathedral was designed by Sir Christopher Wren to dominate the London skyline. Today, though sometimes obscured by larger buildings, it is still a prominent landmark at many points along the Thames. Here it is perfectly framed by the twin towers of Cannon Street station, which are virtually all that remain of the original Victorian buildings, as the body of the station has been replaced by a 1960s office and shopping complex.

Golden mosaics and intricate carving

Wren enlisted the services of some of the finest craftsmen of the day for the interior of St Paul's. Grinling Gibbons, England's finest woodcarver, worked on the choirstalls, while he and Jean Tijou collaborated on the choir screens. The gilt mosaics above the choir are by several Victorian artists, including G F Watts.

Dirt of ages past

The Vintners, it seems, were a fastidious bunch if the customs still observed on their annual procession from their headquarters in Upper Thames Street to the Church of St James, Garlickhythe are anything to go by. Delicate nosegays are carried to disguise any noxious odours, while a sweeper is employed to walk ahead of the procession to prevent any of the members stepping in something unpleasant; both traditions reflect the squalid state of the streets in medieval times. The company's headquarters, Vintners' Hall, visible from the Thames, was built in 1671.

Brandy Nan

The statue of Queen Anne surveying the traffic of Ludgate Hill is in fact a late Victorian copy of the 1712 original by Francis Bird, which was commissioned to celebrate the completion of St Paul's Cathedral. Anne was renowned for her predilection for spirits, and a satirist of the time coined a cruel ditty about the statue: 'Brandy Nan, Brandy Nan, you're left in the lurch, Your face to the gin shop, your back to the church.'

Globe number three

In 1599 the first Globe theatre opened its doors to the paying public, with works by – and starring – leading dramatist William Shakespeare. Plays such as *King Lear* and *Othello* drew the crowds, but in 1613 an audacious use of props during a performance of Shakespeare's *Henry VIII* led to the thatched roof catching light when cannons were fired; the building was razed to the ground. Royal munificence and public subscription combined to ensure that the theatre reopened the following year. The Puritans closed and demolished this building in the 1640s, but phoenix-like the theatre has once again risen from the ashes. This miraculously faithful recreation of the old building is close to its original site.

*L*ONDON'S DARKER PAST
SOUTHWARK BRIDGE TO TOWER BRIDGE

As the Thames approaches the whimsical, Gothic span of Tower Bridge and prepares to leave the historic heart of London, it passes monuments which stir memories of some of the darker and more tragic episodes in the capital's history.

Here the original Roman town of Londinium began, near the site of London Bridge, the first crossing point of the Thames. Here, too, the ancient medieval city stood, but next to nothing now remains – all was swept away by the Great Fire of London, recalled by Wren's famous Monument, visible from the river.

Just downstream is one of the city's most famous landmarks – and one of the few medieval buildings to survive the fire – the Tower of London. With its terrible history as a place of imprisonment, torture and execution, it is reputed to be the most haunted building in the country.

HMS *Belfast*, now gently rocking at anchor in the river's tidal flow, recalls more recent conflicts.

Wartime heroine

When completed in 1939, HMS *Belfast* was the largest cruiser ever built for the Royal Navy. Named after the port where she was built, she played a vital part in the D-Day landings of 1944 before the scrapyard beckoned in 1971. Her new role as a floating museum saved her from such an ignominious fate and she now houses several exhibitions including a recreation of life below decks in 1943.

A fiery reminder

Known simply as the Monument, Sir Christopher Wren's 61.4-metre (202-feet)-high Doric column is the tallest isolated stone pillar in the world. It was completed in 1677, eleven years after the Great Fire of London which it commemorates. The baker's shop in Pudding Lane where the inferno started was exactly 202 feet west of the site of the column, which is topped by a flaming urn of gilded bronze. The viewing platform, a wearying 311 spiral steps above ground level, yields superb views of London and beyond.

Technological insights

Tower Bridge has become one of London's leading tourist attractions, offering magnificent views from its elevated walkways and an intriguing insight into the workings of a bascule bridge. The machinery required to lift the two huge sections of roadway, or bascules – raised to allow tall vessels passage – was powered by steam until 1976; now it is electrically powered.

Church of many uses

Southwark Cathedral is the oldest Gothic church in London, although the thirteenth-century tower constitutes most of its visible medieval fabric. The church has a chequered history – part of it has been used as a bakery and even as a pigsty – but recent centuries have been kinder to the building, with secular use now including the more respectable pastime of classical music recordings.

Baroque splendour

Traditionally the church of fishmongers, St Magnus the Martyr stands at the north end of London Bridge, between Fishmongers' Hall and the old Billingsgate Market. In his poem *The Wasteland*, T S Eliot describes the 'inexplicable splendour of Ionian white and gold' of its gilded baroque interior.

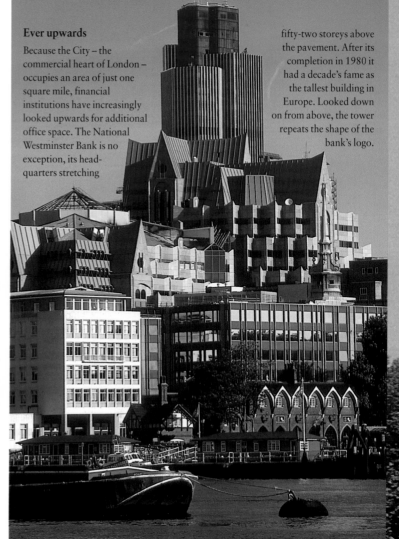

Ever upwards

Because the City – the commercial heart of London – occupies an area of just one square mile, financial institutions have increasingly looked upwards for additional office space. The National Westminster Bank is no exception, its headquarters stretching fifty-two storeys above the pavement. After its completion in 1980 it had a decade's fame as the tallest building in Europe. Looked down on from above, the tower repeats the shape of the bank's logo.

DOGGETT'S COAT AND BADGE RACE

Thomas Doggett, an eighteenth-century Irish comic actor and theatre manager, was so impressed by the skills of the Thames watermen that he instituted a rowing contest in their honour. Started in 1715 to mark the first anniversary of the accession of George I, the race has been held every year since, and is reckoned to be the longest continuously contested boat race in existence. On or near 1 August, depending upon the state of the tide, six watermen set off in sculls from London Bridge and race down the river to the finishing post at Chelsea Bridge. The winner is awarded a scarlet coat and a special badge. Since Doggett's death in 1721, the responsibility for the race's organisation has lain with the Fishmongers' Company, one of the oldest and richest of the City livery companies whose Fishmongers' Hall is beside the Thames.

Doggett's coat and badge

Thomas Doggett

A secure tradition

'An escort for the keys!', shouts the Chief Yeoman Warder, a distinctive figure in scarlet coat and Tudor bonnet, clutching the keys of the Tower of London. By way of response four armed soldiers march forward and together they make their way around the fortress locking the towers. The Ceremony of the Keys repeated every night at about 10pm, is one of England's oldest traditions, having barely changed in over 700 years.

Farewell to freedom

The infamous Traitors' Gate afforded the last glimpse of the free world for many a condemned prisoner brought by river to languish in the Tower.

Mighty stronghold

The most perfect medieval fortress in Britain, the Tower of London has remained almost intact throughout its bloody history, a grim fortified stronghold brooding beside the Thames, the gates in its massive walls still locked every night. Today it offers protection to some of Britain's most valuable treasures, the Crown Jewels, but for most of its history it has been a place of imprisonment, torture and execution. The list of those who met their deaths in the Tower's precincts is chillingly long; its last prisoner was the Nazi leader Rudolf Hess, held here for four days during the Second World War.

Ceremony of the Keys

Traitors' Gate

Towards the Sea

TOWER BRIDGE TO GREENWICH AND THE THAMES BARRIER

The character of the Thames changes dramatically as it leaves Tower Bridge behind, the river growing ever wider as it flows towards the sea. In the eighteenth and nineteenth centuries vast docks, quays and warehouses were built here, and the river was crowded with all kinds of vessels. But when trade moved to the huge container port of Tilbury on the Thames estuary, the Victorian docks were abandoned. Only in the last couple of decades has commercial activity resumed here, albeit of a very different kind.

The area marketed as Docklands, a prime site for brave new office developments, is a fascinating mixture of post-modernist constructions, converted warehouse apartments and chic new housing projects, interspersed with the occasional proud remnant of an earlier era. And amidst all this stands noble Greenwich, its naval college a living monument to the human relationship with the sea, its maritime museum a reminder of England's glorious seafaring history. Further on still is the Thames Barrier, a miracle of engineering ingenuity, giving protection from the sea's tides to the great conurbation of London.

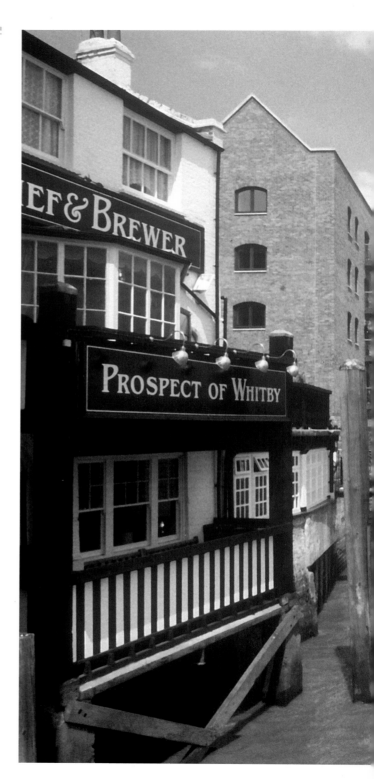

A historic watering-hole

According to local legend, the Prospect of Whitby pub was once the haunt of thieves and smugglers and was originally known as the Devil's Tavern. Built in 1520, it is one of the oldest pubs on the river. In 1777 it was renamed after a ship called the *Prospect*, registered in Whitby, which brought stone to London and habitually moored just outside the tavern.

Tall ambitions

A monument to the optimism of the enterprise culture of the 1980s, the main tower of the Canary Wharf development, Canada Tower, rises some 250 metres. This makes it the tallest building in the United Kingdom and the second tallest office block in Europe.

A nautical flavour

Dwarfed by the Docklands office blocks, St Mary's Church, Rotherhithe, stands close to the Thames and is very much a seamen's church. Its construction in 1705 was entirely funded by the parishioners of Rotherhithe, mainly sailors and watermen, and the nautical associations are tangible: the piers are built from ships' masts thinly encased in plaster, while an altar table and two bishop's chairs are formed from the timbers of the *Téméraire*, a veteran warship of Trafalgar.

Pioneering redevelopment

St Katharine's Dock, designed by Thomas Telford in 1828, handled exotic cargoes from the East, including live turtles for soup. By the 1960s it had become derelict, but an ambitious redevelopment scheme in 1973, which included a marina, gave it a new lease of life.

HAUNT OF THE HANGING JUDGE

Only in the 1980s was Wapping transformed into a district of smart office complexes and expensive apartments. Centuries ago its narrow streets of dilapidated houses were crowded with sailors, fishermen, smugglers and pirates, and it was a notoriously dangerous place.

It was a favourite drinking haunt of the infamous seventeenth-century 'hanging judge', Judge Jeffreys, who also frequented a pub on the opposite bank of the river from where he could get a good view of Wapping's execution dock. This grisly spot, now marked on the quayside with the letter E, was where seafaring criminals, pirates and smugglers were hanged at the low-water mark – and then left until three tides had washed over them. Among them was Captain Kidd, the celebrated pirate.

Legend has it that in a Wapping pub, the Town of Ramsgate, Jeffreys was captured on the point of escaping to France after the overthrow of James II. Though in disguise, he was recognised by a lynch mob from whom he had to be rescued by a company of soldiers. Imprisoned in the Tower of London, he later died of drink.

Small but significant

Perched on the hillside beyond the imposing pillars and pediments of the Royal Naval College are the little buildings of the Old Royal Observatory. The scientific research carried out here ensured that the name of Greenwich would become famous the world over. In 1884 the Greenwich Meridian was universally accepted as 0° longitude, the division between eastern and western hemispheres, and it is marked by a brass rail running through the courtyard of the Old Royal Observatory. In the same year Greenwich Mean Time became the basis of time measurement for most of the world, recorded on the observatory's magnetic clock.

Classical simplicity

When Inigo Jones was commissioned to design the Queen's House (*right*) at Greenwich in 1616, he was presented with an unusual challenge – to accommodate within the royal palace the muddy Deptford to Woolwich road which ran straight through the site. He solved the problem by designing the house in two halves linked by a bridge over the road. The result, against all the odds, is one of the most perfect Palladian buildings in the country. Though the road was subsequently diverted, its course is still marked in the cobbles of the courtyard.

Sumptuous ceiling

The ceiling of the remarkable Painted Hall in the Royal Naval College took Sir James Thornhill twenty years to complete, and represents a dazzling mixture of myth, history, allegory and reality. This was to have been the pensioners' dining room, but was in fact only used by the pensioners on very special occasions. In 1806 Nelson's body lay in state here for three days, while enormous crowds filed by to pay their respects.

Perfect in every detail

The 'House of Delights' was how Queen Henrietta Maria, wife of Charles I, described her house at Greenwich. Though the exterior is austerely classical, Inigo Jones allowed himself 'licentious imaginacey' in designing the interior, shown not least in the exquisite Tulip Staircase, so called after the graceful floral motifs in its ironwork.

An ancient history

There has been a church on this site since 1012, the year in which St Alfege, Archbishop of Canterbury, was murdered at Greenwich by Danish invaders. The present building, dedicated to the eleventh-century saint, is largely the work of the great church architect Nicholas Hawksmoor; its fine steeple is visible from the river, just beyond the *Cutty Sark*.

Queen of the tea-clippers

London to China in just 107 days was a world record when the famous clipper *Cutty Sark* raced home in 1871. Then she was the fastest ship of her time, carrying precious cargoes between London and the Orient. Today she rests in dry dock at Greenwich, a proud monument to the great age of sail. A visit on board reveals the cramped conditions in which her sailors lived, and among the maritime memorabilia is a fine collection of painted ships' figureheads.

Hospital turned college

The magnificent Royal Naval College at Greenwich began life as a charitable institution. It was conceived by the monarchs William and Mary in the late seventeenth century as a hospital for retired seamen, housing almost 3,000 pensioners. For 150 years the old men in their blue coats with yellow linings were an integral part of the riverside scene, but eventually the noble scheme was judged a failure. The pensioners, it seemed, were not happy in their sumptuous surroundings: discipline was harsh and they complained about the food. The hospital became the Royal Naval College in 1873.

A problem solved

Fourteen people were drowned in their Westminster basements in 1928, and the 1953 flood accounted for over 300 fatalities further east. To the high-tech rescue of London has come the Thames Barrier, complete with shining armour. Finished in 1982, it is the largest moveable flood defence in the world and stretches over 500 metres across the river at Woolwich. Ten huge gates of steel can be raised in under thirty minutes, and in their first thirteen years of operation they have held back the surge tide on more than twenty occasions.

THE DEMISE OF THE DOCKS

Until comparatively recently the Thames has been a busy, dirty, crowded route for goods to and from the world's foremost trading nation. Even within living memory its lower reaches were crowded with vessels of all descriptions – great ocean-going passenger liners jostled for space with cargo carriers, launches, tenders, dredgers, excursion steamers, sailing barges, lighters and tugs.

The first secure, enclosed dock with adequate warehousing – the West India – was built in 1802 and throughout the nineteenth century the marshy land east of Tower Bridge was gouged out into a series of ever larger dock complexes. But only a few decades after the last dock was built, in 1921, vessels had almost ceased to use the Thames and by the 1960s the great docks lay empty and abandoned. The busy atmosphere of the old docks has been replaced by the clean, streamlined, mechanised procedures of the new container port of Tilbury at the river's mouth.

Entrance to London docks

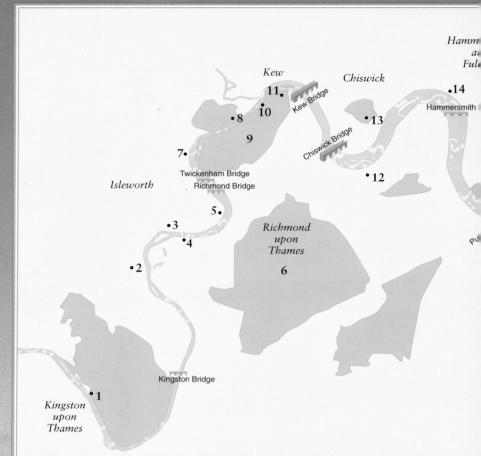

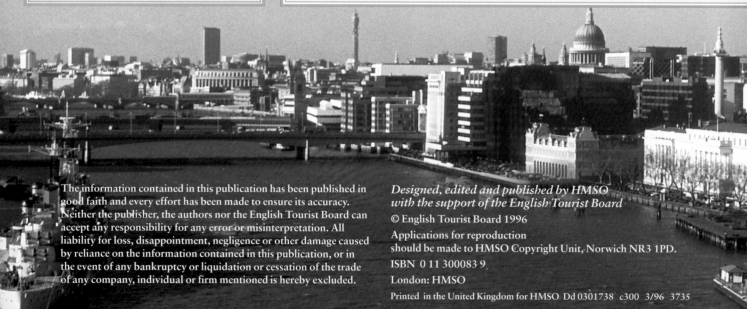

Designed, edited and published by HMSO with the support of the English Tourist Board

© English Tourist Board 1996

Applications for reproduction should be made to HMSO Copyright Unit, Norwich NR3 1PD.

ISBN 0 11 300083 9

London: HMSO

Printed in the United Kingdom for HMSO Dd 0301738 c300 3/96 3735